David Robinson

All-Star Center

by

Thomas S. Owens

The Rosen Publishing Group's
PowerKids Press™
New York

Published in 1997 by The Rosen Publishing Group, Inc.
29 East 21st Street, New York, NY 10010

First Edition

Book Design: Kim Sonsky

Photo Credits: Cover © AP/Wide World Photos; p. 6 (left) © FPG International; p. 6 (right) © PhotoDisc; all photos © AP/Wide World Photos.

Owens, Tom, 1960–
    David Robinson : all-star center / Thomas. S. Owens.
        p.   cm. — (Sports greats)
    Includes index.
    Summary: Examines the life and achievements of the first graduate of the United States Naval Academy to play in the National Basketball Association.
    ISBN 0-8239-5091-3
    1. Robinson, David, 1965– —Juvenile literature. 2. Basketball players—United States—Biography—Juvenile literature. 3. Centers (Basketball)—Juvenile literature. 4. San Antonio Spurs (Basketball team)—Juvenile literature. [1. Robinson, David, 1965– . 2. Basketball players. 3. Afro-Americans—Biography.]
    I. Title. II. Series: Sports greats (New York, NY)
    GV884.R615094 1997
    796.323'092—dc21   97-4153
                                                                      CIP
                                                                      AC

Manufactured in the United States of America

Contents

A Scary Start

When David Robinson was six months old, his parents weren't thinking about him becoming a basketball star. They just wanted him to be alive and healthy. One day, David's mother took him to visit his aunt. She laid him down on a bed, and left the room for just a moment. David accidentally rolled off the bed. When Mrs. Robinson came back, David was trapped against the wall by the mattress, and had stopped breathing. Mrs. Robinson was a nurse, so she knew how to help him breathe again. Still, he had almost died. His family worried that he would never be healthy.

◀ David Robinson may have had a scary start, but he went on to become a strong, healthy basketball star.

Sports ... Sometimes

Thankfully, David was unhurt from the accident. He grew up smart and strong. Born on August 6, 1965, David was reading at age three. As early as first grade, he was taking classes for gifted students. In elementary school, David liked science fiction books and **electronics** (ee-lek-TRON-iks) as much as sports. David did well at all sports, including tennis, golf, and gymnastics. The five-foot, nine-inch David tried playing basketball in eighth grade, but quit the next year because it took time away from homework! He seemed happier taking math and computer classes at a nearby college.

David liked playing basketball, but he also liked studying math and learning to use the computer. ▶

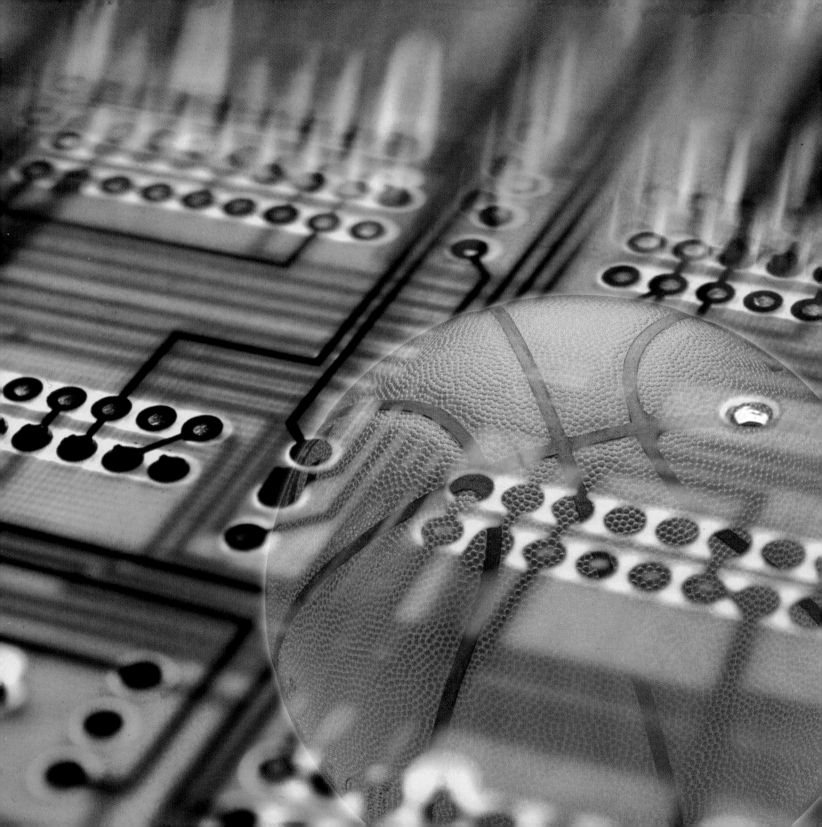

Growing Up and Up!

When David started his senior year of high school, he had grown to be six feet, seven inches tall. David's family had just moved because his father had **retired** (ree-TYRD) from the Navy. David was at a new school in a new town. The basketball coach took one look at David and wanted him on the team. The coach didn't care that the tall, new kid didn't know a lot about the sport. He talked David into joining anyway. David's team wasn't great. They won twelve games and lost twelve games. David was still more interested in homework than basketball. So, rather than looking for a college where he might become a future basketball star, David went to the **Naval Academy** (NAY-vul uh-KAD-eh-mee) to study electronics.

David went on to become a star on the Navy's basketball team.

9

NBA

School or Sports?

David played basketball at the Academy. During his second year, he grew to be six feet, eleven inches tall. His team won the **conference** (KON-frents) title. They went to the National Collegiate Athletic Association (NCAA) **tournament** (TER-nuh-ment) for the first time in 25 years. David knew he was good enough to play **professionally** (pro-FESH-un-ul-lee). But he was faced with a tough choice. If he stayed at the Naval Academy, he would have to be an officer in the Navy when he finished school. If he changed to a different college, he could play for the National Basketball Association (NBA) at any time. David decided to stay at the Academy.

10

In 1985, David won an award for being college's basketball player of the year. ▶

Can David Play?

The San Antonio Spurs got to pick first in the 1987 draft. A draft is when teams take turns choosing **amateur** (AM-uh-cher) players from schools and other countries. Newspaper reporters wrote that no teams would choose David Robinson, even though he was such a good player. David would have to serve up to five years in the Navy after college. Reporters guessed that teams would choose players who could start right away. To everyone's surprise, David was the first player picked. But the Navy got David first. Would the Navy let him play part-time, or not at all?

◀ Basketball fans across the country wondered whether the Navy would let David play part-time.

13

No Time to Practice

The Navy said David could serve for two years rather than five. David was now seven feet, one inch tall. The Navy knew that such a tall person wouldn't fit well on airplanes or in submarines. But the Navy said David must serve as an officer every day during those two years. He couldn't play part-time. **Lieutenant** (loo-TEN-unt) Robinson worked at a Naval base in Georgia. There, he was in charge of building docks for big ships to stop at when they came to shore. David did get time off to play in the 1988 Olympics. But because David didn't have time off from his job to practice basketball, he didn't play as well as he could have in the Olympics.

14

Although David couldn't play with his NBA team until after he finished working for the Navy, he ▶ was allowed to play in the 1988 Olympics.

Life in the NBA

Two years later, David was in the NBA. He didn't waste time proving that he was worth the wait. David's first game was on November 4, 1989. Playing the position of center, he helped his little-known Spurs. With 23 points and 17 rebounds, the team beat superstar Magic Johnson and the Los Angeles Lakers, 106 to 98. David's first year was nearly everything the fans had hoped. He was an All-Star, and **Rookie** (ROOH-kee) of the Year. Best of all, the Spurs won 35 more games than they had the year before without David. That was a record the whole team could share.

◄ David knew he made the right choice by choosing to play professional basketball.

17

Move Over Michael

When Chicago Bull's superstar Michael Jordan retired in 1993, David stepped into the spotlight. He led the **league** (LEEG) in scoring, averaging almost 30 points per game. In a game against the Los Angeles Clippers in 1994, David scored 71 points. This was a team record. He played on gold medal-winning Olympic "Dream Teams" in 1992 and 1996. He was the first male basketball player to play in three Olympic Games. When the NBA had its 50th anniversary in 1996, reporters voted on the top 50 players from the past 50 years. David made that team too!

David took center stage when Michael Jordan retired. ▶

David's Neighborhood

As well as being a great basketball player, David is also a good actor. He has starred in many funny **commercials** (kum-ER-shulz) by Nike, a sports-shoe company. David pretended to be like Fred Rogers, the star of public television's "Mr. Rogers' Neighborhood," and was called "Mr. Robinson." His neighborhood was a basketball court. But David wasn't pretending when he played the piano in a commercial. And he's not that different from his "Mr. Robinson" **character** (KAYR-ek-ter). He speaks quietly and kindly when talking about teammates, other teams, and fans.

David was so popular that there was a candy bar named after him. Many students sold these candy bars to help raise money for their schools, clubs, or projects.

21

Off the Court

When the Spurs travel, David likes to bring his keyboard. He can also play the saxophone. David says he dreamed of being a musician or a scientist when he was young. He likes math, and enjoys building and fixing things. He likes to play golf, and holds a tournament each year to raise money for many **charities** (CHAYR-ih-teez). His parents are proud that David cares about others. They wrote a book called *How to Raise an MVP: Most Valuable Person*. In sports and in life, David **deserves** (dee-ZERVZ) that title.

22

Glossary

amateur (AM-uh-cher) A person who does something for fun, not for money.

character (KAYR-ek-ter) A person in a play, poem, story, book, movie, or commercial.

charity (CHAYR-ih-tee) A group that looks after the sick, the poor, or the needy.

commercial (kum-ER-shul) A message selling something on television or the radio that is played during and between programs.

conference (KON-frents) An organization of sports teams.

deserve (dee-ZERV) To be worthy of or have a right to.

electronics (ee-lek-TRON-iks) The branch of science that studies tiny particles called electrons.

league (LEEG) An organization of sports teams.

lieutenant (loo-TEN-unt) A rank of office in the Navy. A person's work in the Navy depends on his or her rank.

Naval Academy (NAY-vul uh-KAD-eh-mee) A school where students learn about how to build and run ships.

professionally (pro-FESH-un-ul-lee) Something that you are paid to do.

retire (ree-TYR) To stop working or using something.

rookie (ROOH-kee) A first-year player.

tournament (TER-nuh-ment) A game or games made up of many people or teams, often in a sport.

23

Index